THE KIDS' LIBRARY OF MARTIAL ARTS™

JU JITSU

Pamela Randall

The Rosen Publishing Group's
PowerKids Press™
New York

Published in 1999 by The Rosen Publishing Group, Inc.
29 East 21st Street, New York, NY 10010

First Edition

Book Design: Danielle Primiceri

Photo Illustrations by Seth Dinnerman.

Randall, Pamela.
    Ju jitsu / Pamela Randall.
        p.   cm.—(Martial arts)
    Includes index.
    Summary: Introduces the history, basic moves, and terminology of this martial art.
    ISBN 0-8239-5235-5
    1. Ju jitsu—Juvenile literature.   [1. Ju jitsu.]   I. Title. II. Series: Randall, Pamela. Martial arts.
    GV1114.R36   1998
    796.815—dc21   97-49269
                                                                              CIP
                                                                               AC

Manufactured in the United States of America

Contents

Brittany and the Bully

At school last week, a bully started a fight with Brittany. The boy didn't hit her, but he hurt her with his words. Brittany was scared.

Brittany's brother, Mark, said, "You should take ju jitsu with me so you won't be so scared."

"Ju jitsu will help me stand up to someone?" Brittany said.

"Yes and it's a lot of fun," Mark said.

Brittany decided to start taking ju jitsu lessons with her brother.

◀ *Signing up for lessons in any of the martial arts can be very exciting.*

The Gentle Martial Art

There are many ways to spell the Japanese **martial art** (MAR-shul ART) called ju jitsu, including jiu jitsu, ju jutsu, and ju jutso. There are many styles of ju jitsu too. Some styles use only **throws** (THROHZ), while others include kicking and hitting.

Ju jitsu is called the gentle art, but it isn't always gentle. There are ju jitsu moves that can really hurt an **opponent** (uh-POH-nent). Usually, though, students will just try to make their opponents fall.

Students of ju jitsu learn to overpower opponents ▶
without the use of weapons.

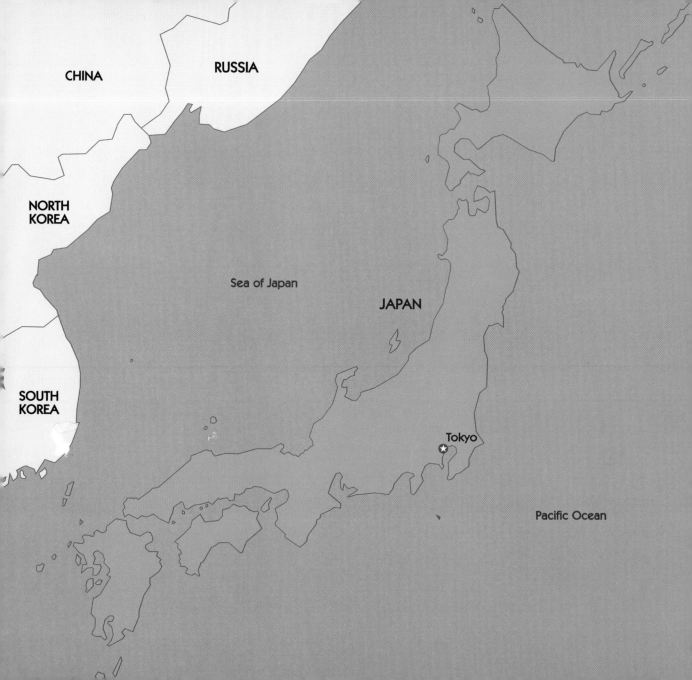

Ancient History

Ju jitsu is a very old martial art. One Japanese **legend** (LEH-jend) tells of two ancient gods, or beings greater than humans, named Kashima and Kadori. They used ju jitsu moves on their enemies.

People have used ju jitsu moves for a long time. But they weren't always called ju jitsu until Hisamori Takenouchi set up the Takenouchi *Ryu* (REEYOO) in 1532. *Ryu* means school. That school was the beginning of the empty-handed, or without weapons, moves that people who practice ju jitsu do now.

◀ *Ju jitsu was created in Japan, which is part of East Asia. All martial arts began in East Asia.*

Strength Doesn't Count

One Japanese legend says that a form of ju jitsu was created in the 1600s by Shirobei Yoshitoki Akiyama, a doctor who studied martial arts. One winter day, he watched snow falling on tree branches. The branches of big trees broke under the snow's weight. But the willow tree's thin branches bent under the weight and sprang back, throwing off the snow. Akiyama knew then that strength isn't always the most important thing. He made up moves, later called ju jitsu, that allow **flexible** (FLEK-sih-bul) people to defeat stronger opponents.

Being flexible is an important part of ju jitsu and most martial arts. ▶

Samurai

In Japan in the 1500s, there were fierce **warriors** (WAR-ee-yurz) called **samurai** (SA-muh-ry). Along with swords and knives, the samurai used ju jitsu when fighting their enemies.

By the 1800s many things had changed in Japan. The samurai found that they weren't needed because there were fewer wars being fought. They began teaching ju jitsu to townspeople to earn money. The townspeople and the samurai weren't allowed to carry weapons. People felt they needed ju jitsu for **self-defense** (SELF-dih-FENS).

◄ *With moves such as this one, called* Ippon Se Nage, *people are able to defend themselves without weapons.*

Modern Ju Jitsu

Around the same time that the samurai were teaching ju jitsu to local people, a young man named Jigaro Kano began studying ju jitsu in 1860. He wanted to learn ju jitsu so that he would grow stronger. Indeed, he grew very strong in body and mind. In fact, Jigaro Kano created some new moves of his own. He gave a name to the mix of ju jitsu and his own moves: judo. This is why ju jitsu and judo are so much alike.

If students master their moves, they can defeat ▶ opponents who are bigger than they are.

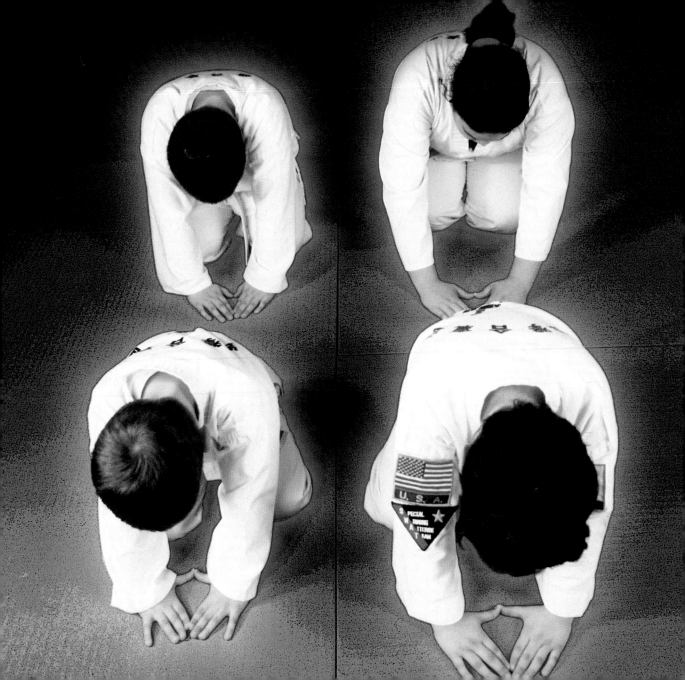

Manners and More

At **traditional** (truh-DIH-shun-ul) **dojos** (DOH-johz), students are taught rules of **etiquette** (EH-tih-kit). This is why opponents bow to each other out of **respect** (ree-SPEKT) before they **spar** (SPAR). Students of ju jitsu learn more than manners so there are many reasons people study ju jitsu. Ju jitsu teaches self-defense and builds **self-confidence** (SELF-KON-fih-dens). And while people who practice ju jitsu grow stronger over time, they don't have to be big and strong to master most of the moves.

◀ *Ju jitsu involves more than learning moves and sparring. Students must follow the rules of the dojo and show their instructor and fellow students respect.*

Dressing Right

Most ju jitsu students wear a *judogi* (JOO-doh-GEE) when they practice. Some even wear a long split-skirt called a *hakama*. Sometimes people have to use ju jitsu for self-defense when they are wearing normal clothes. Because of this, students are able to practice moves in street clothes as well.

Along with their *judogi*, students wear belts around their waists. These belts show a student's rank or skill level. Beginners wear white belts. Students in the highest ranks wear black. Students in middle ranks wear belts of yellow, orange, green, purple, or brown.

Ju jitsu moves can be done in any kind of clothes. It is easiest ▶ to practice in loose-fitting clothes, such as a judogi.

A Ju Jitsu Move

As Brittany takes lessons, she will learn many different moves. One of them is the One-Hand Same Wrist Grab. This move is used if someone grabs one of her wrists with one of his hands.

She pulls her wrist free by twisting toward her opponent's thumbs. Brittany and her classmates will practice this move many times. Then they will be able to do the move without even thinking about it.

Mirror Fighting

Brittany and Mark practice their ju jitsu moves at home. Mark tries out his punches, kicks, and body movements while watching himself in the mirror. Brittany pretends that someone is attacking her from behind. She moves the way she's been taught to avoid a real attacker.

Brittany won't learn to defend herself in just a few lessons. But she feels safer knowing that one day she'll be able to defend herself. And with every lesson, Brittany is building more self-confidence.

Glossary

dojo (DOH-joh) A school where ju jitsu is practiced.

etiquette (EH-tih-kit) The rules for behavior most people follow.

flexible (FLEK-sih-bul) Being able to stretch and bend your body in many different ways.

judogi (JOO-doh-GEE) The uniform worn when practicing ju jitsu.

legend (LEH-jend) A story from the past that many people believe.

martial art (MAR-shul ART) Any of the arts of self-defense or fighting that is practiced as sport.

opponent (uh-POH-nent) A person who is on the other side in a fight or a game.

respect (ree-SPEKT) To think highly of someone or something.

ryu (REEYOO) A school or style of ju jitsu.

samurai (SA-muh-ry) A kind of warrior that worked for the ruling class of Japan up until the twentieth century.

self-confidence (SELF-KON-fih-dens) A firm belief in oneself and one's abilities.

self-defense (SELF-dih-FENS) To protect yourself against an attack.

spar (SPAR) To have a practice fight.

throws (THROHZ) A move that causes someone else to fall.

traditional (truh-DIH-shun-ul) When something is done in a way that was passed down through a family or a culture.

warrior (WAR-ee-yur) A person who fights in a war.

Index